100
FASCINATING
BIBLE
FACTS

Randy Petersen

Publications International, Ltd.

Randy Petersen is a freelance writer with more than 40 books to his credit, including *Bible Fun Stuff, The Family Book of Bible Fun,* and *Praying Together.* He is director of Bible education at his Methodist church in New Jersey.

ACKNOWLEDGMENTS:
Unless otherwise noted, all Scripture quotations are taken from the *New Revised Standard Version* (NRSV) of the Bible. Copyright © 1989, by the Division of Christian Education of the National Council of the Churches of Christ in the USA. Used by permission. All rights reserved.

Quotations marked KJV are taken from *The Holy Bible, King James Version.*

COVER CREDIT: Shutterstock.com

CONTENTS

❧ A NEW WORLD ❧ TO EXPLORE

*T*HE BIBLE opens up new worlds for its readers. In its pages, we meet heroes and healers, prophets and pilgrims. Most important, we find people who know God, who need God, who love and learn from him.

The stories of Scripture happened in a different time and place. The books of the Bible were written over a span of more than a thousand years, and the last book was written 1,900 years ago. Many of the customs seem strange to us today. Much of the history is obscure. That's why any serious Bible reader needs to be a learner. You can't assume that Moses or Ruth or David or Mary was just like you. Their world was different. They ate different foods, lived in different kinds of houses, and spoke different languages. To understand them, we need to understand their culture.

That's where this book comes in handy. While *100 Fascinating Bible Facts* will certainly help you dazzle your friends at the next church potluck, the greater benefit is this: It will help you navigate the biblical world in an informed way. The more you explore the ancient customs, the more you can identify with the people of the Bible. And as you identify with them, you can learn what they learned. You can pray with them and praise with them. God can be as real to you as he was to them.

Within these pages, you'll find a storehouse of information with answers to many of your questions about the Bible. Discover a cornucopia of scriptural facts pertaining to people, animals, plants, temples, synagogues, languages, customs, and, of course, the Bible itself.

So enjoy this book. Play games with it. Read one fact a day, and look up the verses it references. Let it liven up your family dinners. But more than anything, let it draw you into new worlds. Let it crack open a door into God's dealings in human history. Learn as much as you can with your head, but also with your heart.

⚘ ABOUT THE BIBLE ⚘

GENESIS: BOOK OF ORIGINS

THE WORD genesis means "beginning," so you might expect the Bible's first book to deal with origins, and it does. How did the world begin? How did human beings enter the scene? How did sin make its debut? All of these beginnings appear in the first few chapters.

In chapter 12 the attention turns to Abraham, the father of the Jews. He represents another kind of beginning: the origin of the Hebrews. Genesis follows Abraham from his Babylonian roots to the Promised Land of Canaan, continuing the story with his son, Isaac, and twin grandsons, Jacob and Esau. Jacob's 12 sons became the patriarchs of the tribes of Israel.

The last quarter of Genesis tells of Joseph, Jacob's favorite son, who was sold into slavery by his jealous brothers. He rose to prominence in Egypt and later his brothers joined him there. Genesis ends with the Israelite clan in Egypt. How did they get back to their Promised Land? You can find that answer in the next book of the Bible, Exodus.

READING BACKWARD

⟨✦⟩

N THE ORIGINAL Hebrew of the Old Testament, words are often placed out of their natural order to produce a special effect. We find one dramatic example in Genesis 6:9, which reads, "Noah walked with God." The name *Noah* is actually found at the end of the sentence, for emphasis: "With God walked Noah."

Here's another striking detail. When the Hebrew letters of Genesis 6:9 are read backward, the name *Enoch* is revealed. Who was he? One chapter earlier we read that Enoch also "walked with God" (Genesis 5:24).

⟨✦⟩

EXODUS: A WAY OUT

⟨✦⟩

HE WORD *exodus* means "a way out." So, as you would guess, the book by that name is an escape story. Specifically, this second book of the Bible tells how the Israelites left Egypt.

At the burning bush, God called Moses to tell Pharaoh, Egypt's ruler, to release the Hebrews. After ten plagues, Pharaoh agreed, but then changed his mind and sent his army after the fleeing Israelites. It took a miracle of major proportions—the parting of the Red Sea—to ensure the safety of God's people.

Exodus also includes the Ten Commandments, given at Mount Sinai. The last half of the book contains details of the great Covenant Code of Laws, as well as instructions for building the tabernacle—the tent where God would dwell as his people traveled across the desert.

WHO WAS EL SHADDAI?

ONE OF GOD'S titles was *El Shaddai*, usually translated as "God Almighty." The word *el* is a generic term for a god, used by various Semitic cultures at that time. So the God of Israel had to identify himself by various modifiers—God Most High (*El Elyon*), God Who Sees (*El Roi*), God Eternal (*El Olam*) and quite often *El Shaddai*, God Almighty.

In one fascinating exchange, God told Moses that he had appeared to Abraham, Isaac, and Jacob as *El Shaddai*, but now he was introducing himself by his personal name, *Yahweh* (Exodus 6:3).

THE PARTING OF THE WATERS

THREE TIMES the Bible mentions waters being miraculously parted. Many know that the Red Sea divided when the Israelites needed to cross it, because an Egyptian army was hot on their heels. But the Jordan River also parted—twice. After wandering for 40 years in the desert, Joshua led the Israelites within sight of the Promised Land. The river was the final obstacle. God ordered the priests to carry the Ark of the Covenant into the river, and when their feet hit the water, the flow stopped. Once again, the entire nation crossed a river "on dry ground" (Joshua 3).

There's one more account of the Jordan parting. Nearing the end of his earthly life, the mighty prophet Elijah took his protégé, Elisha, down to the Jordan. Elijah rolled up his cloak and struck the water with it. The water parted, allowing these two men of God to cross (2 Kings 2:7–8).

THE TEN COMMANDMENTS

*T*HE BIBLE has lots of laws. Two-and-a-half books are crammed full of regulations on everything from manslaughter to skin disease. But at the beginning of all those laws (Exodus 20), and at their heart (Deuteronomy 5), we find the Ten Commandments. The rest of the laws expand upon these universal moral principles.

God inscribed the Ten Commandments on tablets of stone, which Moses brought down from Mount Sinai (Exodus 34:28;

Deuteronomy 4:13; 10:4). Some modern folks bristle at the negativity of the Ten Commandments—all those "Thou shalt nots." But these boundary lines provide a moral standard for any healthy society.

THE 611 COMMANDMENTS

*T*HE JEWISH rabbis counted 611 separate commandments in the Law of Moses. Of those, 365 of them (one for each day of the solar year) were stated negatively, and 246 positively. In Hebrew, each letter of the alphabet corresponds to a number. Significantly, the word *Torah*, Hebrew for "law," has a numerical value of 611.

THE LAW OF LOVE

*T*HE STORY sounds like a modern press conference. At the height of his popularity, Jesus was grilled by tough interviewers sent by his enemies. They were trying to trap Jesus with trick questions. One of them backfired. "What is the greatest commandment in the Law?" they challenged. That's a bit like asking, "Which of your children do you love most?" God gave all the laws. If Jesus chose "Do not murder," would that mean he was soft on adultery? Whatever commandment he chose, they would have an opportunity to skewer him for neglecting others.

His reply was brilliant. "You shall love the Lord your God with all your heart, and with all your soul, and with all your mind." Then he added a second commandment—"You shall love your neighbor as yourself"—declaring that all the Scriptures hang on these two laws (Matthew 22:37–40).

Many know that Jesus summed up God's laws in those two sayings. What many don't realize is that Jesus was only quoting the Old Testament. The first commandment is found in Deuteronomy 6:5 and the second in Leviticus 19:18.

SYMBOLIC NUMBERS

MANY NUMBERS had symbolic value in the Bible. The number *one* symbolized God's unity. "The Lord is one," declares Israel's best-known statement of faith (Deuteronomy 6:4). Later, in Christian thinking, *three* came to symbolize the Trinity.

From the start, *seven* was a number of completion and perfection. For example, God rested on the seventh day of creation, when his work was completed. The psalmist compares the promises of God to silver refined in a furnace, "purified seven times" (Psalm 12:6). Since there were *12* tribes of Israel, it's no accident that Jesus chose 12 disciples. That's also the symbolism behind the 12 gates of the New Jerusalem (Revelation 21:12).

Biblical events often unfolded in *40s.* Noah's flood took 40 days and nights. The Israelites wandered for 40 years. Jesus spent 40 days fasting in the desert and in his resurrected state before his ascension.

HALLELU-YAH!

*T*HE WORD *hallelujah* is Hebrew for "praise the Lord." It contains a shortened form of God's name: *Yah* (for Yahweh). You can see the same thing in the names of many biblical characters, with *jah* or *iah* at the end. The Hebrew form of Hezekiah is *chizqi-yah*—"Yahweh is my strength." Isaiah is *yesha-yahu,* "Yahweh saves." Elijah means "my God is Yahweh," and Nehemiah is "Yahweh comforts." From Adonijah ("My Lord is Yahweh") to Zechariah ("Yahweh remembers"), scores of biblical Israelites incorporated God's name with their own.

LARGE SYMBOLIC NUMBERS

*W*HEN PETER asked Jesus how many times he should forgive his brother, he probably thought that seven was plenty. Seven symbolized completeness, so it would only make sense that forgiveness would run its course after seven offenses. Jesus however, replied, "I tell you, seventy-seven times" (Matthew 18:21–22). Some translations have "seventy times seven," but the idea is the same. When you want a big symbolic number, start multiplying.

The number 70 took on the same sense of completion that seven had—only on a larger scale. Israel had 70 elders and endured 70 years of captivity in Babylon. At one point Jesus sent out 70 disciples.

The number 1,000 symbolized something indefinitely large, as in "With the Lord one day is like a thousand years" (2 Peter 3:8). Twelve is also an important number, so putting 12 and 1,000 together had a strong symbolic meaning. For example, we see the 12s appearing in combination with 1,000 in Revelation, where 144,000 is the number of saints sealed up to God (Revelation 7:4; 14:1)—that is, 12 times 12 times 1,000.

MEDIEVAL COPYISTS

N THE YEARS before scanners and photocopiers, how were Bibles copied? Very carefully. Jewish scribes and Christian monks painstakingly reproduced page after page by hand, with stringent rules to preserve the accuracy of the text. (Sometimes, as a way of proofreading, the numerical value of the letters on each line was tallied.) During the Middle Ages, copying became an art form, with elaborate calligraphy and colored inks used in manuscripts. Occasionally the copyists also drew tiny, beautifully detailed pictures in the margins and at the beginning of chapters.

THE SEPTUAGINT

LEXANDER THE GREAT had a short career as a world conqueror, but it made a long-lasting impact. He swept through the Middle East, carrying the Greek culture with him. By the third century B.C., the Greek language was commonly spoken in cities throughout the region. Pockets of Jews lived in these cities, having migrated in times of famine and war. Increasingly, they spoke Greek rather than Hebrew, and that created a problem. How were they to read, study, and teach the Hebrew Scriptures?

Legend has it that 72 translators (representing six from each tribe of Israel) convened in Alexandria, Egypt, in about 250 B.C. to create a Greek version of the Scriptures known as the *Septuagint* (which means "70"). Most modern scholars date its translation later and estimate that it took place over a longer period of time. But the Septuagint was certainly being used by the Apostle Paul's time, allowing him to preach about Jesus from prophetic Scriptures to audiences of both Jews and Gentiles.

THE HEBREW BIBLE: DIFFERENT ORDERING

THE HEBREW BIBLE is the same as the Old Testament in the Christian Bible, right? Well, yes. It has the same books, but in a different order. The Hebrew Scriptures have three sections: the Law (*Torah*), the Prophets (*Nabiim*), and the Writings (*Kethubim*). The first five books are the same as in the Christian Bible, the five books of Moses. Then comes the Prophets, with the same basic major/minor grouping as the Old Testament (based on length of the books), but this section also includes some historical books, such as Joshua, Judges, and the double books of Samuel and Kings. The Writings contain the Psalms and other poetic books that the Old Testament has in the middle, but it also has the book of the prophet Daniel and some historical books, ending with 2 Chronicles.

When Jesus talked about "the law and the prophets" (Matthew 5:17), he was using a common phrase of the time that referred to all of the Hebrew Scriptures. It's unclear why the third part was left out of that phrase, but it's possible that the Writings were seen as the work of prophets.

JOB: QUESTIONS ABOUT INNOCENT SUFFERING

THE BOOK of Job is not an employment manual. It's one of the world's classics on the question of human suffering. Job (the name rhymes with *robe*) is described as "blameless and upright, one who feared God and turned away from evil." It would seem that, due to his faith and righteousness, he should have lived a life of prosperity. And he did—until God decided to take it all away. Job lost his home, his wealth, his family, and his health, all because of a wager God made with the devil. And while he passionately questioned God, Job never abandoned his faith.

As Job sat on the ash heap, scraping his sores, friends came by to comfort him and to analyze his suffering. For 30-odd chapters they challenged the poor man, thinking he must have done *something* to deserve this misfortune. Finally, God spoke up, declaring how he had created the universe. But God never really answered Job's question. Why all this suffering? His response was basically, "I'm God, and you're not."

Eventually, Job got back everything he lost, and more. His story teaches us a valuable lesson about staying faithful even when we don't understand what God is doing.

PHANTOM BOOKS

*T*HE BIBLE often refers to books that no longer exist. After describing one of Joshua's exploits, the text says, "Is this not written in the Book of Jashar?" (Joshua 10:13). Well, who on earth is Jashar? Apart from two references to his book, we have no clue about this historian.

The same thing occurs with references to writings such as *The Book of the Wars of the Lord, The History of the Prophet Nathan,* and *The Visions of the Seer Iddo.* Where are these books? It's possible that parts of them are included in the Old Testament books—obviously they were being used as resources—but it seems the complete works have been lost.

Closing his letter to the Colossians, Paul suggests that they swap this epistle with the one he sent to the church in the next town over, Laodicea. Fine, except that the Laodicean epistle has been lost to history too. (However, some scholars think the Colossians did just as Paul asked, copying the Laodicean epistle and merging it with their own, so what we now know as Colossians includes both letters.)

In the New Testament, Jude cites a strange legend about the archangel Michael arguing with the devil over the body of Moses. Scour the Old Testament, and you won't find that story. It's in a book written between the Testaments, *The Assumption of Moses.*

APOCALYPTIC LITERATURE

*D*OES THE BOOK of Revelation puzzle you? Join the club. Many modern readers have trouble fitting in the Bible's last book with the Gospels and epistles. What sort of writing was John doing?

It was actually a form of writing familiar to John's first readers. From about 200 B.C. to A.D. 100, a number of works appeared on similar themes, addressing the end times. These writings were rich with symbolism, making them tantalizing to read, but difficult to interpret precisely. Often claiming to be the results of dreams and visions, they were heavily populated with angels and other spiritual beings. Scholars refer to this genre as apocalyptic literature.

Other sections of the Bible that might be considered apocalyptic include Ezekiel 40–48, Daniel 7–12, and Zechariah 9–14.

THE HANDWRITING ON THE WALL

*T*HE NEXT TIME you hear someone mention "the writing on the wall," take a look at Daniel 5, where the phrase originated. The Babylonian king Belshazzar was giving a lavish feast, and the guests were drinking from the holy vessels that had been looted from the Jerusalem Temple. Suddenly the king saw a hand writing words on the wall. Terrified, he asked his advisors to interpret the graffiti. Only Daniel could.

The message consisted of four cryptic words, *Mene, Mene, Tekel, Peres.* They appear to be amounts of money, as if it were saying, "Dollar, dollar, penny, half-dollar." But each word had a root meaning, which Daniel used in his interpretation: *numbered, numbered, weighed, divided.* Belshazzar's days were numbered; his kingdom wasn't worth its weight; so it would be parceled out to other nations.

That very night, the handwriting on the wall came true. The Medo-Persian empire conquered the Babylonians, and Belshazzar died.

WHICH DAY IS JESUS' BIRTHDAY?

*N*OWADAYS PEOPLE start preparing for Christmas in October. But is December 25 really Jesus' birth date? We don't know.

We do know that December 25 was the accepted date of Christmas by the early A.D. 300s, and possibly earlier. In the Roman Empire, December 25 was the day of the Mithraic festival of the sun god (it's near the winter solstice, when the sun is highest in the sky). Christians took this date as an opportunity to turn a pagan festival into a Christian one. The Eastern Church celebrates Christmas on January 6, traditionally the date of the Magi's visit, but the exact date of Jesus' birth is unknown.

WHO WERE THE MAGI?

*T*HE GREEK historian Herodotus (fifth century B.C.) spoke of Magi, a priestly tribe in the Persian Empire. Was this the background of the wise men who visited the baby Jesus? Perhaps.

We know very little about the Magi of the Christmas story. They are identified as "from the east," which could mean Persia, Arabia, India, or beyond. Since they followed a star, we might associate them with the star scholars of Babylonia. Some have suggested that they followed a tradition started in Babylonia (and Persia) by the Jewish prophet Daniel, who made a name for himself as an interpreter of strange dreams.

The word *magi* is used later in the New Testament to mean magicians. (That's where we get the word *magic.*) But the Magi who saw Jesus seemed more interested in divine direction than in parlor tricks. By the way, Scripture doesn't say there were three Magi on that journey. That assumption comes from the three gifts they brought: gold, frankincense, and myrrh.

"*ABBA*, FATHER"

*W*OULD YOU CALL GOD "Daddy"? That's what Jesus did.

Shortly before his arrest in the Garden of Gethsemane, Jesus began a prayer with "*Abba,* Father" (Mark 14:36). The Aramaic word *abba* is an intimate form of the word *ab,* which means "father." It was an informal term of intimacy and respect used by children, something like da-da or daddy.

The Apostle Paul picked up on the idea when he said that "God has sent the Spirit of his Son into our hearts, crying, 'Abba! Father!'" (Galatians 4:6; see also Romans 8:15). Does "Daddy" seem too informal? No—that's exactly Paul's point. We are not mere slaves, he says, but the very children of the Father.

THE EARLIEST BIBLICAL TEXTS

SCHOLARS PORE over ancient texts to see what the books of the Bible originally said, but even the earliest manuscripts they have are copies of copies. Archaeologists keep digging to find earlier sources, closer in time to the actual writing. But papyrus crumbles; many ancient works have been lost, burned, or buried.

In 1979, alongside the Scottish Church in Jerusalem, excavators found two beautiful silver amulets. These date from about the time Jerusalem was overrun by the Babylonians in 587 B.C. What made this find so special was the words inscribed on the amulets: the priestly benediction known as the Aaronic Blessing, seen in Numbers 6:22–27. That makes these artifacts the earliest biblical texts in existence today.

A SECRET PASSWORD

*Y*ou've seen the fish outline on car bumper stickers. You probably know it's a Christian symbol. But where did it come from? What does it mean?

It's actually a very early symbol of Christianity, used as a code word. The Greek word for fish is *ichthus*, and way back in the Roman Empire, Christians saw that word as an acronym that could stand for Jesus. (An acronym uses the first letter of each word in a phrase to form a new word.) So the Christians could refer to their Lord as "Jesus Christ, God's Son, Savior," and the Greek acronym would form like this:

I *(iota)*	I*esous*	Jesus
CH *(chi)*	CH*ristos*	Christ
TH *(theta)*	TH*eou*	God's
U *(upsilon)*	(h)U*ios*	Son
S *(sigma)*	S*oter*	Savior

When Christians were being persecuted by the Romans, they could use *ichthus* as a password, keeping their religious identities secret. The symbol even appears in some of their underground meeting places.

✌ LANGUAGE ✌ AND LITERATURE

A Is for Ox

*T*HE EARLIEST ALPHABETS were based on picture-languages. Perhaps you've seen early Egyptian hieroglyphics, where the symbols were pictures of the words they represented, such as birds or snakes. The Hebrew language represents a later step, where letters of an alphabet stood for certain sounds. But those letters were often shaped like common objects whose names started with those letters. The first letter of the Hebrew alphabet is the *aleph*, derived from *alpu* ("ox"), and so the first *aleph* was a line drawing of an ox head. (And through a series of linguistic steps, it is the ancestor of the English capital A.) The second letter, *beth*, is squared off with an opening at one side, something like a house. The word *beth* means "house."

JOTS AND TITTLES

*J*ESUS SAID, "One jot or one tittle shall in no wise pass from the law, till all be fulfilled" (Matthew 5:18 KJV). What was he talking about? The "jot" was the *yodh*, the smallest letter

24

of the Hebrew alphabet, equivalent to our letter *i*. The "tittle" was only part of a letter, a small pen stroke—something like the dot over an *i* or the crossing of a *t*. Modern translations get the idea right when they say, "not one letter, not one stroke of a letter, will pass from the law" (NRSV).

THE ALPHA AND THE OMEGA

EIGHT VERSES into the Book of Revelation, the Lord God says, "I am the Alpha and the Omega." That has caused a few beginning Bible students to scratch their heads. What is God saying about himself?

Alpha and *omega* are the first and last letters of the Greek alphabet. So the Lord was declaring his presence at the beginning and the end of human history. Just as the Bible's first book starts, "In the beginning, God . . . ," this last book of Scripture places God at the end of time as well.

The phrase "I am the Alpha and the Omega" occurs twice more, in the last two chapters of Revelation, uttered by "the one who was seated on the throne" (presumably God the Father) and by Jesus, who adds "the first and the last, the beginning and the end" (Revelation 22:13; see also 21:6; 1:8).

ASHURBANIPAL'S LIBRARY

THE KING OF ASSYRIA put together a library with more than 26,000 volumes. Located in the capital city of Nineveh, this structure had separate rooms for collections of history, religion, and science. These works were carefully catalogued. Amazingly, this library was built in the seventh century B.C.

Ashurbanipal was ruler of the mightiest empire on earth at the time. Assyria had already swept away the ten northern tribes of Israel. But along with his military exploits, this king proved to be the greatest patron of literature in the pre-Christian Era. His library contained government documents (in a secret chamber), but it wasn't just an archive for old files. Ashurbanipal commissioned his emissaries to search the world and bring back copies of every known text.

Much of what we know today of ancient Mesopotamia comes from the 1853 discovery of this library.

SCAPEGOAT OR DEMON?

DID YOU KNOW that the word *scapegoat* comes from the Bible? Leviticus 16 describes a ritual involving two goats. One was sacrificed to the Lord as a sin offering, but the other was allowed to live, released into the desert after Israel's sins were symbolically transferred onto its head. The King James Version calls the escaped animal the "scapegoat," and much later that term entered the English language for anyone who takes the blame for others.

Recent scholarship, however, suggests a different translation. The Hebrew word for scapegoat, *azazel*, was probably the name of a desert demon. Under this interpretation, the goat was sent "to Azazel" to remove Israel's sin completely.

THE LANGUAGE OF JESUS

WHAT LANGUAGE did Jesus speak? Aramaic, which is closely related to Hebrew. Greek was the common language spoken throughout the Mediterranean world, and traditional Hebrew was used in Scripture study and worship, so Jesus would have known those languages, but in daily life he would have used Aramaic. A few Aramaic words and phrases are preserved in the Gospels—when Jesus prays, "*Abba*, Father" or when he summons a little girl (*talitha*) back from the dead—but most of the New Testament was written in Greek.

Aramaic all but died out in later centuries, but amazingly it's still spoken today in isolated villages of Syria, Turkey, Iran, and Iraq.

WHAT IS ANTI-SEMITIC?

*N*OWADAYS, IF someone is called "anti-Semitic," it means they're prejudiced against Jews. However, the word actually has a much broader meaning.

The term *Semite* comes from Noah's oldest son, Shem, referring to races that were historically considered his descendants. That group would include both Jews and Arabs, who are actually very close to each other in race and language. So technically both Jews and Arabs are Semites, and anti-Semitism would mean opposition to all those of Middle-Eastern ethnicity.

ANCIENT WORDS OF WORSHIP

*Y*OU MAY KNOW more ancient Hebrew than you realize. In fact, you've probably used the language in worship. A number of words from Hebrew (and the closely related Aramaic) have become part of Christian church services through the centuries.

Hallelujah means "Praise the Lord!" Look closely, and you'll see the short form of God's name, *jah* (short for *Jahweh* or *Yahweh*), attached to the Hebrew word for praise.

Hosanna is often heard in Palm Sunday services, since it was shouted during Jesus' Triumphal Entry into Jerusalem. Originally meaning "save us," it was the sort of welcome you'd give to a victorious general riding in to free your city from oppressors.

Amen is Hebrew for "surely," "so be it," or just plain "yes!" It has long been uttered at the end of prayers, but Jesus often used it at the beginning of key teachings. " *Truly, truly,* I say to you … "

Maranatha was an Aramaic word meaning "Our Lord, come!" The Apostle Paul exclaimed this as he anticipated Christ's return to earth (1 Corinthians 16:22).

PAPYRUS: EARLIEST PAPER

*P*APYRUS WAS an early, inexpensive material used as a writing surface. Our word *paper* comes from *papyrus*. This plant is a long reed that grows especially in the marshes of the Nile River. In ancient times papyrus was used for fuel, food, and even clothing. The baby Moses was floated down the Nile in a little boat made of papyrus (Exodus 2:3). But its greatest use was in writing, through an ingenious process the Egyptians probably developed.

Reeds were cut down, stripped of their bark and laid in rows. Then another layer was placed on top, crosswise, and the two layers were pounded together. After it dried, it produced a reasonably smooth writing surface. Sometimes sheets of papyrus would be joined together in scrolls. Later they were bound in books. One benefit to archaeologists: Because the dry climate of the Middle East preserves papyrus quite well, many ancient documents are still readable.

A Living Language

THE HEBREW BIBLE, or Old Testament, was written over a period of 1,000 years, primarily in Hebrew. As you might expect, the language changed a great deal over that time.

Toward the end of the Old Testament period, Hebrew actually began to die out as a spoken language, partly as a result of the Jews' intermarriage and assimilation with other cultures. We see this in Nehemiah's distress over Jews who had married foreigners and whose children could not even speak "the language of Judah" (Nehemiah 13:23–24).

By Jesus' day, most Jews in Israel spoke Aramaic, a Syria-based language similar to Hebrew. Those Jews who had scattered throughout the Mediterranean world spoke Greek and perhaps local dialects. This becomes apparent in the response of the crowd at Pentecost (Acts 2:6–11). These Jewish pilgrims were visiting Jerusalem from many different cities, but it took a miracle for all of them to understand the same language.

For more than 2,000 years, Hebrew was kept alive only among rabbis. Then, about 100 years ago, Eliezer Ben-Yehuda, a Lithuanian Jew, worked tirelessly for its revival as a spoken language. Certainly the establishment of the nation of Israel, and its adoption of modern Hebrew, helped make that a reality. Modern Hebrew is based upon biblical Hebrew and Talmudic Aramaic, and it has traces of German and Russian.

SAVE THAT BROKEN POT!

ONE CULTURE'S trash is another's treasure. During biblical times, many short documents were written on pieces of broken clay bowls or pots, which today's scholars highly prize. These potsherds were just the right size on which to jot a quick letter or note to someone or perhaps to write a receipt or bill. The writing was done with pen or brush and ink.

THE SUMERIANS: THE FIRST LITERATES

*T*HE BOOK OF GENESIS gives us few details about life before Abraham, but archaeology has filled in some of the blanks. For instance, we read in Genesis 10:10 about the land of Shinar. This might be another name for Sumer, a nation that dominated the region of the Tigris and Euphrates in the third millennium B.C.

As far as we know, the Sumerians were the world's first literate people. They invented the writing of cuneiform, triangular symbols pressed into wet clay with a reed stylus. They composed many texts, including great mythological epics and moving love poetry. One king of Sumer, Ur-Nammu, left a law code considered the world's earliest. Another Sumerian text describes a victory of the city of Lagash over the city of Umma—this is the world's oldest text using sequential sentences.

One of the major Sumerian cities was Ur. We find it in Genesis as the home of Abraham, before God led him to Canaan.

AN EGYPTIAN REFERENCE TO ISRAEL

*A*NCIENT KINGS loved to boast about their victories. The pharaohs of Egypt were especially good at this. They often set up monuments inscribed with the names of their vanquished foes. For archaeologists, these inscriptions provide excellent opportunities to cross-check the names and dates of neighboring nations.

It's on one such monument that we find the earliest reference to Israel outside the Bible. It dates to about 1208 B.C. After following Moses out of Egypt, the Israelites settled in the land of Canaan. But the Egyptian pharaoh Merneptah apparently launched a successful attack against them—or at least he claimed he did. In a victory song carved in stone, he boasted about all the enemies he had defeated, including Israel: "Israel is laid to waste, his seed is not." Subsequent history proves he had exceedingly overstated the case.

WHAT IS A BAR MITZVAH?

*A*T THE AGE OF 12, Jesus traveled with his family to Jerusalem, where he met with rabbis. Many readers assume that this was his *bar mitzvah*. The term is Hebrew for "son of the commandment." In Judaism today, when a boy reaches his 13th birthday, a ceremony is held declaring him an adult, now responsible for his own religious life. At this public celebration, the boy reads a portion of the Torah and usually expounds on a religious topic.

However, the custom of a bar mitzvah celebration arose only a few centuries ago. (The custom of a bat mitzvah for girls—*bat* means "daughter"—has also arisen recently in Judaism.) So it's unlikely that Jesus' boyhood journey involved such a ceremony.

THE SALT COVENANT

MANY FOLKS routinely add salt to their meals as a seasoning. Would it surprise you to know that the sacrifices of the Israelites were also seasoned with salt? "You shall not omit from your grain offerings the salt of the covenant with your God," the law says; "with all your offerings you shall offer salt" (Leviticus 2:13). Salt was also included in the incense used in worship (Exodus 30:35).

The Bible also mentions a "covenant of salt." This was apparently an agreement sealed with a sacrificial meal that involved salt. Since salt was a preservative, it symbolized eternity. A salt covenant would be preserved forever. When God stipulated that priests and Levites should receive sacrificial meat, he confirmed it with a salt covenant (Numbers 18:19). The second salt covenant mentioned in Scripture involved the granting of Israel's throne to David and his descendants (2 Chronicles 13:5).

666: The Number of the Beast

On June 6, 2006, some people were bracing for an onslaught of evil. Why? The date was 6/6/6, and that number is described in Revelation 13:18 as "the number of the beast."

There has been endless speculation about the interpretation of that number and the identity of "the beast." As John describes it, the beast—often called the Antichrist—is an evil figure who deceives the world and dominates it. Many early interpreters thought individual Roman emperors were being referred to, perhaps Nero or Domitian. Various methods of assigning numbers to letters have been attempted. In the second century, Irenaeus saw the number as symbolic of all evil, and many modern interpreters concur. Being one digit short of the triple number of perfection—777—the number could symbolize the way evil falls short of God's standard of perfection.

Love by Any Other Name

The Greek language has three major words for love. *Eros* denotes sexual love. Though common in classical Greek, this word is never found in the New Testament. *Philia* denotes married love or a close friendship. It was exalted as an ideal in Greek culture. *Agape* was rarely used in classical Greek, but it's the most common word for love in the New Testament. The biblical writers adopted this word as their own, using it for God's love and the love his people show for him.

WHITEWASHED TOMBS

*J*ESUS PULLED no punches in criticizing the Pharisees. Their pride and hypocrisy made them fair game. In Matthew 23, Jesus called them blind fools, snakes, a brood of vipers. And in one especially striking metaphor, he compared them with whitewashed tombs, "which on the outside look beautiful, but inside they are full of the bones of the dead and of all kinds of filth" (verse 27).

It was an apt charge. Many of the Pharisees worked overtime to appear righteous to others, but their hearts were selfish and corrupt. According to Jewish law, touching a dead body made a person unclean, and so some tombs actually were whitewashed so that people wouldn't accidentally come in contact with them.

ANIMALS AND PLANTS

A Whale of a Tale?

Contrary to popular belief, a whale probably didn't swallow Jonah. This prophet's fateful journey was in the Mediterranean Sea, where whales are rarely sighted today and may have been unknown in biblical times. The Book of Jonah merely mentions a "great fish" as the prophet's temporary refuge. When Jesus referred to the story, he used an old Greek word for a large sea monster (Matthew 12:40).

BIBLICAL ANIMALS

The Bible mentions dozens of animals, wild and domestic, in many different contexts. Almost 180 Hebrew terms and more than 50 Greek terms are used for animals. But these words pose special difficulties for translators. Occasionally the Bible gives us detailed descriptions of certain creatures, but in many cases animals are merely listed. And if an animal name appears only once or twice and seldom in works outside the Bible, translators have no context with which to work. In addition, some animals have become extinct since biblical times, so there's no modern equivalent. As a result, not all the terms can be identified with certainty, and translators use considerable guesswork.

***

UNICORNS IN THE BIBLE?

YOU MIGHT be surprised to skim through the Bible and find unicorns. These magical one-horned horses are creatures of myth, right? And yet the King James Version of the Bible mentions unicorns nine times, in ways that make them sound very real. What's going on?

Actually, those passages refer to the oryx, a magnificent, white horselike creature with two long, straight horns. It was hunted almost to extinction in the nineteenth century. Today, this animal is slowly being restored in Israel by wildlife conservationists.

***

BALAAM'S DONKEY

WHAT IF your pets could talk? What would they say about how they're treated? No, that's not a pitch for a Disney movie. It actually happened to a biblical prophet named Balaam.

He was a strange character from the beginning. Balaam had prophetic power from God, but he was sort of a freelancer. He was hired by Balak, an enemy of Israel, to utter a curse against Israel. God told him not to do it, but Balaam saddled up his donkey anyway and headed out to meet with Balak. When an angel blocked the road, the donkey saw it and veered off the path. Apparently Balaam was blind to the angel, because he beat the donkey, ordering it to move forward. This happened twice more, and finally the donkey was fed up.

"What have I done to you, that you have struck me these three times?" the donkey asked. The man and the beast had a brief conversation before Balaam saw the angel and got things squared away with God (Numbers 22:1–35).

UNEQUALLY YOKED ANIMALS

ON MANY farms in ancient times (as well as modern times), animals were used to help with the chores. A donkey could pull a wagon. An ox could pull a plow, using its strength to drag the instrument through the hard earth. When the earth was especially hard, or when there was a lot of ground to cultivate, a pair of oxen could be teamed by placing a yoke over their necks. This double harness, usually made of wood, kept the oxen side by side, ensuring that they would plow straight and efficiently.

Farmers who didn't have two oxen might be tempted to yoke an ox together with a donkey. However, the Law of Moses prohibited this practice (Deuteronomy 22:10). Why? There might be several reasons. Practically speaking, the mismatched animals would not plow a straight furrow. More importantly, the law was humane, since both animals would struggle with the uneven yoke.

But there's a moral lesson in here too. The commandment is placed among various rules about not mixing things. Don't plant different kinds of seed in the same field. Don't wear clothes that mix wool and linen. Many Old Testament laws are about separating the Israelites from the heathen nations around them. The Lord wanted his people fully committed to him, not halfhearted in their devotion.

In the New Testament (2 Corinthians 6:14), the Apostle Paul alludes to the yoking command when he says, "Do not be mismatched with unbelievers" (the King James version has "unequally yoked").

CROCODILES

ROCODILES CRAWLED around the Nile River in biblical times, as they do now. Do they appear in Scripture? Maybe.

Old Testament poetry includes references to a creature named Leviathan. Isaiah calls Leviathan "the twisting serpent . . . the dragon that is in the sea" (27:1). And an entire chapter of Job is devoted to describing it, with a series of rhetorical questions. "Who can penetrate its double coat of mail? Who can open the doors of its face? There is terror all around its teeth. Its back is made of shields in rows" (41:13–15). Later verses mention "the folds of its flesh." These detailed descriptions lead many scholars to think that Leviathan is in fact the crocodile of the Nile.

EAGLES

AGLES ARE mentioned more often than other birds of prey in the Bible. Their great size, strength, speed, and soaring ability make them perfect material for divinely inspired metaphors. When the Lord reminds the Israelites how he rescued them from the Egyptians, he says, "You have seen . . . how I bore you on eagles' wings and brought you to myself" (Exodus 19:4).

41

As David lamented the deaths of Saul and Jonathan, he called them "swifter than eagles" (2 Samuel 1:23). The speed of eagles was a point of comparison for the swift armies of an enemy, the fleeting days of our lives, and the temporary quality of riches (wealth suddenly "takes wings . . . , flying like an eagle toward heaven"—Proverbs 23:5).

Perhaps most stirring is the message from Isaiah that "those who wait for the Lord shall renew their strength, they shall mount up with wings like eagles" (40:31).

THE FOUR HORSEMEN OF THE APOCALYPSE

REVELATION 6 paints a graphic picture of four magnificent horses and their riders, representing the evils to come at the end of the world.

The first horse is white, representing conquest; its rider carries a bow and wears a crown. The second horse is red, representing war; its rider has a sword. The third horse is black, representing famine; its rider carries a set of scales, indicating the economic catastrophe to come. The fourth and final horse is described as pale; its rider's name is Death. This rider represents war, famine, pestilence, and wild beasts, all at once. (The "pale" color of this last horse is, in Greek, *chloros*, which is actually green, used elsewhere in the New Testament as the color of grass.)

THE TREE OF LIFE

*Y*OU'RE FAMILIAR with the forbidden tree in the Garden of Eden. Adam and Eve were allowed to eat fruit from any tree except one, the Tree of the Knowledge of Good and Evil. But there was another tree mentioned by name in that garden: the Tree of Life (Genesis 2:9). God placed it in the middle of Eden as a symbol of eternal life.

After they sinned by eating from the forbidden tree, Adam and Eve were no longer allowed access to the Tree of Life. The Lord feared a scenario in which the man "might reach out his hand and take also from the tree of life, and eat, and live forever" (Genesis 3:22). That is why Adam and Eve were banished. God did not want humankind to live eternally in sin.

But the Bible's end reclaims its beginning. Revelation describes the tree of life growing in the New Jerusalem, bearing 12 kinds of fruit. Its leaves are used for healing (Revelation 22:2).

AARON'S ROD

*S*HEPHERDS HAD two important tools in Bible times: a rod and a staff. The staff was a long pole, sometimes bent at the end, for prodding and guiding sheep. The rod was a shorter club, often used to defend against predators. We see both of these tools of the trade in the well-known Shepherd's Psalm: "Your rod and your staff—they comfort me" (Psalm 23:4).

Rods had several other purposes: They could be used as measuring sticks or walking sticks, and leaders often held them as symbols of authority. And it never hurt to have a weapon handy.

But the most famous rod in the Bible belonged to Moses' brother, Aaron. In an attempt to impress the Pharaoh of Egypt with the power of God, Aaron threw down his rod, and it turned into a snake. Big deal—the Egyptian magicians duplicated the trick. But then Aaron's snake devoured theirs (Exodus 7:8–12).

On another occasion, there was a showdown with a rebellious faction over priestly authority. Aaron's rod sprouted buds, blossoms, and almonds overnight—God's way of confirming him as the high priest of Israel (Numbers 17:1–11). After that, Aaron's miraculous rod was kept in the sacred Ark of the Covenant.

THE OLIVE BRANCH

*T*HE OLIVE branch is an international symbol of peace. But how did the olive branch acquire that reputation? The imagery might come from the story of Noah (Genesis 8:1–12).

After the rain stopped, the flood waters were still high. Noah sent out first a raven and then a dove to investigate the situation, but water still covered the trees. Then a second dove brought back an olive leaf, indicating that some trees were above water. So the image of the olive branch became connected with the dove in a message of peace and renewal.

THE ROSE OF SHARON

*I*N THE RICH love poetry of the Song of Songs (aka Song of Solomon), a beloved woman compares herself to the "rose of Sharon" (2:1). What was this beautiful flower? It was actually not a rose as we know roses today, but probably a tulip of some kind, either the *Tulipa montana* or the *Tulipa sharonensis*, which grows deep red among the grasses on the Plain of Sharon.

𝒮 TEMPLES 𝒮
AND SYNAGOGUES

THE TEMPLE

𝓑UILT AND REBUILT on a high plateau in Jerusalem, the Temple was a magnificent structure, built by Solomon in about 960 B.C. He retained the finest artisans for the project, employed a huge labor force to quarry and cut the stones, and signed a deal with King Hiram of Tyre to provide cedar wood. Having worshipped in tents for centuries, the Israelites were enthralled with this structure.

You can imagine the devastation, then, when a Babylonian army invaded Jerusalem in 586 B.C., destroying the Temple and looting its sacred artifacts. The Persians allowed the Jews to rebuild it in 516 B.C. Some who remembered the glory of the first Temple actually wept at the plainness of this rebuilt one (Ezra 3:14; see also Haggai 2:3).

Shortly before the time of Jesus, King Herod the Great launched a massive remodeling of the Temple, probably in an attempt to shore up his popularity with the Jews. His successors continued the project through Jesus' time and beyond. In fact, the Temple construction lasted until the Romans utterly leveled it in A.D. 70, an event that Jesus had foretold (Matthew 24:2).

Today, the Islamic Dome of the Rock stands where the Temple once stood.

THE TABERNACLE: PRECURSOR TO THE TEMPLE

WHERE DOES GOD LIVE? Many ancient religions included the sense of "holy space"—sacred temples, mountains, or groves where they worshipped—but the Israelites took it to a new level. They did have a sacred place to worship God, but it was *portable*.

God gave the Hebrews detailed instructions for building a large tent—the tabernacle—that would be moved from place to place as they wandered through the desert. The tabernacle was richly decorated with expensive fabrics, and there was a special place for the Ark of the Covenant and other sacred items.

Years after the Hebrews settled into the Promised Land, worship was transferred to the Temple in Jerusalem, which had a basic structure quite similar to the tabernacle.

THE WAILING WALL

*T*HE JERUSALEM TEMPLE was demolished by the Babylonians, rebuilt, and destroyed again by the Romans, but there's one section of an outer retaining wall from the first-century Temple that King Herod rebuilt. This is the only part of the Temple that remains.

This Western Wall has become a place of prayer. Over the centuries, Jews have visited the Wall to express their grief over the Temple's destruction, the pain of their long exile, and their hope for a return to their homeland. Because so much lamentation and weeping took place at this wall, it became known by non-Jews as the Wailing Wall.

JESUS AND THE TEMPLE

*J*ESUS FREELY MOVED through the Temple and its courtyards. The inner core of the Temple was a place of sacrifice, worship, and ritual, but the outer courtyards were more social in nature. And some did business there. It was in these Temple courtyards that an angry Jesus overturned the tables of the moneychangers and the merchants because they had turned God's house into "a den of robbers" (Luke 19:46).

Along the perimeter of the Temple complex were colonnades, where Jewish scribes and Pharisees taught the law and held their debates. Here, the 12-year-old Jesus impressed the rabbis with his knowledge. In adulthood, Jesus was the rabbi, with eager disciples surrounding him. "Day after day I sat in the Temple teaching," he said at his arrest (Matthew 26:55; see also John 7).

THE SHEMA

*C*REEDS HAVE ALWAYS been important in the Christian faith. At various points in history, some have set down in writing what they believe. Whether the Apostles' Creed, the Nicene Creed, or others, these statements help bring together communities of faith.

Judaism has something like that as well. It's called the *Shema*, and it comes from Deuteronomy 6:4–9. The basic part of it goes like this: "Hear, O Israel, the Lord is our God, the Lord is one [or the Lord alone]."

This classic statement of Israel's monotheism and God's providence has long been an important part of both morning and evening services in the synagogue. Its name is derived from its first word in Hebrew, *shema*, which means "hear." The later sections include the familiar command to love the Lord with all your heart, soul, and mind. "Keep these words . . . in your heart," the next verses add. "Recite them to your children and talk about them . . ." And that's exactly what's happening.

SOLOMON'S TEMPLE

*S*OLOMON DESERVES great credit for building the dazzling Jerusalem Temple, but his father helped a lot. King David made plans and collected materials, though God prevented him from building the Temple because as a warrior he had "shed blood" (1 Chronicles 28:3).

The materials included tons of stone blocks; boards of cedar, olive, cypress, and algum trees; metals including gold, silver, bronze, and iron; fabrics of purple, violet, and crimson; and beautiful arrays of alabaster, antimony, onyx, and all kinds of colored and precious stones.

THE ARK OF THE COVENANT

*T*HE HOLIEST OBJECT in Israel was a 2×4×2 box. The Ark of the Covenant (sometimes known as the Ark of God) was an ornate chest of acacia wood, overlaid with gold, and topped with a golden cover known as the "mercy seat." On this cover were two golden figures of winged cherubs.

The Ark contained the tablets of the Ten Commandments, a pot of manna, and Aaron's rod. It was kept in the most holy place of the tabernacle (and later the Temple). Once a year, on the Day of Atonement, the High Priest would enter this sacred room and sprinkle blood on the "mercy seat," atoning for the people's sins.

It was understood, then, that this was the point where God touched the earth. He met his people at this place of sacrifice. Sometimes the Ark was seen as God's throne, but more graphically it was described as his footstool (1 Chronicles 28:2).

Modern moviemakers must use considerable guesswork when depicting the Ark; it was almost certainly destroyed in the Babylonian invasion of 586 B.C.

DESTRUCTIONS OF THE TEMPLE

ON A MAJOR STREET in Rome, you can still see the Arch of Titus with its carvings that depict the victory of this first-century general, who later became emperor. You'll see images of soldiers defeating an enemy, sacking a city, and carrying off a menorah.

Wait—a menorah? Sure enough, the carving includes the seven-branched lampstand that was part of the Jews' Temple worship. The scene depicted on that arch happened in Jerusalem. Amazingly, through the ages, we can still view this grim snapshot of the looting of the Temple.

The Babylonians had already destroyed the Temple once, razing Solomon's structure in 586 B.C., but it was rebuilt 70 years later and remodeled in Jesus' time. However, a rebel force of Jews took arms against the Romans in the late 60s of the first century, and the Roman response was brutal. General Titus led a force that quelled the rebellion, killed thousands of Jews, and destroyed the Temple in A.D. 70. It has never been rebuilt.

THE SECOND TEMPLE

*T*HE TEMPLE that Jesus knew was first built in 516 B.C. It lacked the magnificence of Solomon's Temple, but it was functional. King Herod and his successors had expanded it into a magnificent structure with many impressive courtyards, chambers, colonnades, and gates.

Predicting his own resurrection, Jesus once said he could rebuild the "temple" in three days. His opponents commented, "This temple has been under construction for forty-six years" (John 2:20). And construction would continue. In all, the Herods' expansion project lasted more than 80 years.

No Gentiles Allowed

ONLY JEWS were allowed to pass beyond the outer courtyard of the Temple, the Court of the Gentiles. Warning signs in Greek and Latin were posted at regular intervals forbidding others to enter on pain of death. Two such notices have been found, engraved on limestone blocks.

This restriction, along with a misunderstanding, sparked a riot in which the Apostle Paul was arrested. He had been seen around town with a gentile friend, Trophimus the Ephesian. When Paul was spotted later in the Temple, his enemies assumed he had brought the Gentile there too. Since Paul was already vilified for welcoming Gentiles into the church, this charge was believable. People "rushed together" and dragged Paul out of the Temple. His arrest by Roman soldiers probably saved his life (Acts 21:27–36).

THE SYNAGOGUE

*W*HEN THE TEMPLE was destroyed in the sixth century B.C., Jews faced a religious crisis. Many had been taken into Babylonian captivity; others had fled; still others remained in Judah, but their place of worship was gone. Where would they meet with God?

The *synagogue* came about as an answer to that question. (The word is Greek for "gathering.") It was a place of public prayer and worship, but it was not a replacement for the Temple. No sacrifices were carried out in the synagogue. Instead, the reading of the Scriptures replaced the sacrifice as the central event of Jewish worship. Over time, each Jewish community established its own synagogue. Even after the Temple was rebuilt, synagogue worship continued in far-flung communities of Jewish emigrants, in the outlying villages of Judea, and even in Jerusalem itself.

By medieval times, synagogues had developed into the educational, civic, and cultural, as well as religious centers of Jewish communities.

WHICH WAY DO I PRAY?

In Jewish custom, a person prays facing Jerusalem, a tradition that goes back many, many centuries. "I will bow down toward your holy temple in awe of you," the psalmist says (Psalm 5:7; see also 138:2). The prophet Daniel made it a custom to pray three times a day toward Jerusalem, even though this practice landed him in a den of lions (Daniel 6). Later, when most Jews lived west of Jerusalem, a decorated plate or plaque would be hung on the eastern wall of synagogues and homes to indicate the proper orientation for prayer. The plate or plaque, and even the synagogue wall itself, was called the *mizrach* (literally "east").

EVERYDAY LIFE IN BIBLE TIMES

THE ISRAELITE FOUR-ROOM HOUSE

FTER THEY SETTLED in the Promised Land, the Israelites distinguished themselves from their Canaanite neighbors in many ways—even in their architecture. Excavators have identified a particularly Israelite kind of house with four rooms. One room was long, running along the back wall. The other three rooms were side by side, each one opening onto the long room. People would enter the house through the middle room, which usually was used as a courtyard.

CHILDREN'S GAMES

HAT DID THE CHILDREN of Bible times do all day to entertain themselves? Actually, quite a few children's toys have been unearthed among the ruins of ancient Israelite towns. These toys include whistles, rattles, marbles, dolls, and toy animals. Israelite children also kept pets, such as birds. Of course, children were expected to help out in the house or farm or family business, but when they weren't working, they danced, sang, and played games in the streets. In 2 Kings 2, we find a band of small boys amusing themselves by making fun of Elisha the prophet. That didn't turn out so well, but another prophet, Zechariah, foresaw a glorious future for Jerusalem that included "boys and girls playing in its streets" (8:5). Even Jesus referred to children singing, dancing, piping, and playing in the town marketplace (Matthew 11:16).

BUILDING MATERIALS

IN OLD TESTAMENT times, what were Israelite houses made of? Mud. Specifically mud bricks, although sometimes rough stones were included. The walls were coated on the inside with waterproof plaster and the floors consisted of hard-packed clay. Wealthier homes had floors paved with smooth stones.

The roofs were generally made from wooden beams laid flat across the walls. These were covered with branches, which provided a lathwork for mud plaster to make a flat surface. It was probably a roof like this that four men "dug through," in order to lower their paralyzed friend in front of Jesus (Mark 2:4).

Priests' Garments

Priests' clothing was colorful and expensive (Exodus 28). Ordinary priests wore a cloth that covered their hips and thighs and a long linen tunic with sleeves. They also wore turbans and beautiful belts made of blue, purple, and scarlet cloth. The high priest wore an ornate breastplate made of gold and expensive linens. This had 12 precious stones on it—one for each tribe of Israel. The hem of the high priest's robe had small bells on it, which jingled as he walked.

Precious Stones

About 30 different types of precious stones are mentioned in the Bible. They include multicolored agates, reddish-purple amethysts, green emeralds, red garnets, clear diamonds, green jade, yellow-brown jasper, blue lapis lazuli, green malachite, white onyx, pale opals, shiny pearls, red rubies, blue sapphires, multicolored topaz, and blue-green turquoise. Archaeologists have discovered many of these valuable stones, often in beautiful settings of gold and silver.

Several Bible prophecies envision the New Jerusalem with precious gems lodged in its gates and walls (Isaiah 54:11–12; Revelation 21:18–21).

MEDICAL DOCTORS IN THE BIBLE

WERE THERE DOCTORS in Bible times? Absolutely. We think of medicine as a modern science, but there have always been those who specialized in the healing arts.

Joseph enlisted doctors to embalm his father, Jacob, in Egypt (Genesis 50:2). In Israel itself, King Asa of Judah sought medical help from doctors when he had a foot ailment (2 Chronicles 16:12).

Paul identified his colleague Luke as a physician (Colossians 4:14). Interestingly, it's Luke's Gospel that notes a woman who came to Jesus for healing "had spent all she had on physicians, [but] no one could cure her" (Luke 8:43). Luke also cites Jesus' proverb, "Doctor, cure yourself" (Luke 4:23).

WHAT IS WINNOWING?

FARMLAND WAS the setting for much of Scripture, so it's no surprise that some of its deepest spiritual messages are described in the language of growing, cultivating, and harvesting. When John the Baptist explained the mission of Jesus, he said, "His winnowing fork is in his hand, to clear his threshing floor and to gather the wheat into his granary; but the chaff he will burn with unquenchable fire" (Luke 3:17). That sums up a latter stage of the harvesting process.

Stalks of grain were cut and taken to a *threshing floor*, where they were crushed *(threshed)*, to break apart the husks from the edible core. (This "floor" was generally a flat surface outside, usually located on high ground, for maximum wind.) *Winnowing* involved using a narrow pitchfork to toss the entire mixture of threshed grain into the air. The empty husks *(chaff)* would blow away in the breeze, and the edible grain would fall back to the floor, to be gathered for storing, selling, or milling.

Scripture often uses winnowing as an image of God's eventual separation of the faithful and unfaithful. The first psalm speaks of the wicked as "chaff that the wind drives away" (Psalm 1:4).

THE STAFF OF LIFE

*M*ANY COMMON PHRASES in our language come from the Bible. The term "staff of life" refers to a dietary staple, such as rice, potatoes, and especially bread. In the biblical world, bread was *the* basic food, to the point that the word *bread* often stands for food in general. Even those on low-carb diets can pray, "Give us this day our daily bread" (Matthew 6:11).

But why would it be compared to a staff? In Bible times, a staff was something to lean on. When walking was the main mode of transportation, a walking stick was a helpful prop. And if your staff broke, you had a problem.

That brings us back to Scripture where, several times, God talks about "breaking the staff of bread," that is, sending famine as punishment for sin (Leviticus 26:26; see also Ezekiel 4:16; Psalm 105:16). The daily supply of food that the people had been leaning on and taking for granted would be kicked out from under them. It's a harsh reminder that God wants his people to lean on him. In fact, Jesus referred to himself as "the bread of life" (John 6:35).

WINE

WINE WAS the most common drink besides water in the ancient Near East. While drunkenness is acknowledged as a problem (Proverbs 20:1; Ephesians 5:18), wine is generally seen in the Bible as something positive, marking joyous celebrations and solemn religious occasions alike. Jesus' first recorded miracle, at the wedding of Cana, was to turn water into wine. And, of course, he used the wine of his last Passover meal to create a new celebration for his followers.

"SALT OF THE EARTH"

HARDWORKING folks are sometimes referred to as "the salt of the earth." It's a strong compliment, signifying a connection to the basics of life. In fact, Jesus first used the phrase with his disciples, not so much about where they came from, but more about the effect they would have on the world.

In ancient times, salt was used as a preservative as well as a seasoning. In times of shortage, it was doled out to soldiers as pay; this is the origin of the word *salary*. When it was plentiful, it was used in paving roads.

Jesus warned his disciples against losing their "saltiness" (Mark 9:50). Strictly speaking, sodium chloride (salt) is a stable compound and does not lose its saltiness. However, most salt in Palestine came from the Dead Sea, where other minerals and sand were mixed with it. The salt could dissolve, leaving a useless, tasteless compound. Perhaps this is what Jesus had in mind. What good is salt if it's not salty? And what good is a Christian without an ongoing commitment to Christ?

MANNA

IMAGINE THAT YOU'VE been wandering in the desert for months. You've run out of the food you packed for the journey. Bugs and berries aren't very filling, so you are famished. Then one morning you wake up and it's snowing. But it's not snow—flakes of bread seem to be falling from the sky. "What is it?" you ask. That's what everyone is asking. Some desperate person takes a chance on eating the stuff, and it's good. It tastes sweet like wafers with honey, and it's filling. You gather in a basketful for your family to feast on.

That's what happened to the Israelites in the desert. They complained of hunger, and God responded with this bread from heaven. They called it *manna*, which is Hebrew for the question they were all asking: "What is it?" The bread did not keep for more than a day, so it was literally "daily bread." They had to trust God for this gift, new every morning. The only exception was the day before the Sabbath: A double portion came down, and it would keep, so they wouldn't have to work on the day of rest.

Scholars have long tried to find a natural explanation for this phenomenon. It's true that certain insects in the Sinai Desert produce manna-like droppings, but not in such great quantities. It must have been a miracle, plain and simple.

Despite God's generosity, the time came when the Israelites got tired of this wonder bread, and they complained again.

THE TRADES

MOST PEOPLE know that Jesus was a carpenter, but what did that involve? Carpenters and woodworkers made homes, tools for farming, and weapons for war. The word used for this trade could refer to other artisans as well. Some became metal workers, shaping tools, weapons, and jewelry.

Other workers toiled in quarries and mines, digging for stone, salt, iron, copper, gold, silver, and other minerals. Another important trade was pottery. Potters used a basic material to create many objects for everyday life. Indeed, broken pottery is one of the most common items found in ancient towns during archaeological excavations.

THE JOB MARKET

THE PRIMARY occupations during biblical times were the ones that provided the basics: food and shelter. Farmers provided food for people to eat. Shepherds and other ranchers provided meat, as well as skins and wool. In coastal areas, fishing was also a profitable enterprise. In general, women prepared and cooked the food, and they made cloth out of animal hair, from this cloth they made clothes and tents. The whole family would participate in the family business.

FISHING

THE LAND of Israel borders the Mediterranean Sea, as well as two major inland lakes and a river. While farming was the major enterprise in the mountains, and herding was plentiful in the grassy foothills, the area around those bodies of water supported a healthy fishing industry (except for the Dead Sea, whose extremely high mineral content made it inhospitable to life).

The Bible talks about various methods of catching fish. Several different types of nets are mentioned. Fishhooks are also mentioned (Isaiah 19:8), as well as the spear and harpoon (Job 41:7).

The Gospels are full of fishing references, since at least four of Jesus' disciples were anglers. On a couple of occasions, Jesus worked miracles that filled their nets to overflowing. (John, an angler himself, tells us that one of these miracles netted exactly 153 fish!)

A CUBIT

GOD TOLD NOAH to build the ark 300 cubits long and 50 cubits wide. A cubit was a common measurement in ancient times, based on the distance from a grown man's elbow to the tip of his middle finger. The standard cubit was approximately 17.5 inches long, while the royal cubit was longer, about 20.5 inches (suggesting that kings had longer arms). That would make Noah's ark about 440 feet by 73 feet, and 44 feet (30 cubits) high, about the size of your average football field.

A Shekel for Your Thoughts

THE SHEKEL was the basic unit of weight in the ancient Near East. It was small, about four-tenths of an ounce. Small shekel weights in various denominations were used to weigh objects on scales. Archaeologists have uncovered many of these measuring weights.

This weight, applied to precious metals like silver, became a standard for money, too. Abraham bought a burial site for Sarah at a price of 400 shekels of silver. David bought land for an altar in exchange for 600 shekels of gold. The shekel is the basic coin in Israel today.

What's a Talent?

HAVE YOU EVER dreamed of having so much money you couldn't carry it all? That's sort of the idea behind Jesus' parable of the talents. In the story, a master gives three servants certain sums of money—in *talents*. The talent was an enormous sum. The Greek *talanton* was a measure of weight that amounted to between 57 and 95 pounds. When applied to gold or silver, one talent was more than 15 years wages for a common laborer.

What do you make in 15 years? Now imagine your boss gives you five times that amount to invest however you see fit. That's the premise of Jesus' parable.

Here's a case where the Bible has directly contributed to the English language. Bible interpreters have long understood that Jesus isn't just referring to money in this parable. God has given each person abilities—now what will we do with them? Through this common interpretation, the word *talent* came into the English language—not as a sum of money or a weight, but as an ability God has given.

ANCIENT BATHS

WASHING AND bathing were done in all biblical periods for religious and health reasons. The Greeks and Romans introduced large public baths, and many remains of these baths have been found throughout the Mediterranean region. Archaeologists believe a ritual bath facility adjoined the Temple complex in Jerusalem in Jesus' time. That way worshippers could prepare themselves.

Jesus healed a man by the Bethesda Pool in the northeast corner of Jerusalem. This pool supposedly had healing properties. On another occasion, Jesus gave sight to a blind man and told him to wash in the Pool of Siloam, on Jerusalem's south side.

THE STAR OF DAVID

*T*HE SIX-POINTED star of David is a symbol of Judaism, even appearing on the Israeli flag. But does it really go back to King David? Not that we know of. The simple design, with two inverted triangles, was seen in architecture as early as the A.D. 200s, but not in a distinctly Jewish context. Throughout medieval times, both Jews and non-Jews used the star for decorative and magical purposes. Only in modern times was it claimed as the symbol for the Jewish nation.

In Hebrew, it is called *magen David*, "the shield of David," but no evidence supports the legend that it was emblazoned on David's shield. One tempting theory holds that the Hebrew letter *dalet* (D), was shaped like a triangle in David's time, and thus the "star of David" combines the first and last letter of his name.

✌ PEOPLE AND GROUPS ✌

WOMAN AND MAN

*Y*OU PROBABLY noticed at an early age that the word *woman* contains the word *man*. The same thing is true in Hebrew. The word for woman, *ishshah*, contains the word for man, *ish*. According to Genesis 2:23, this is no accident. "This one shall be called Woman (*ishshah*)," Adam sang, "for out of Man (*ish*) this one was taken."

ADAM: EARTH CREATURE?

*M*AYBE WE should call him "Dusty." The name of the first man, Adam, is related to the Hebrew word for earth or soil (*adamah*). Undoubtedly this is an intentional play on words, since Adam was formed from "the dust of the ground" (Genesis 2:7). To emphasize this fact, some modern works translate *Adam* as "earth creature" or "earthling."

The psalmist makes this reference: "He [God] knows how we were made; he remembers that we are dust" (Psalm 103:14).

EVE: MOTHER OF LIFE

*A*DAM HAD an unusual task: He had to name his wife. He was, of course, the namer of all the creatures in Eden, and he had already established the generic terms for man (*ish*) and woman (*ishshah*). But, after they left Eden, he must have envisioned a world full of other men and women, their own children and children's children. She would need a name of her own.

Genesis says, "The man named his wife Eve, because she was the mother of all living" (3:20). In fact, Eve's name in Hebrew (*chavvah*) sounds like the word for "living" (*chayyah*).

SHORTENED LIFE SPANS

*T*HE FIRST 11 chapters of Genesis sweep through millennia of human experience. In between the stories of Eden, Cain and Abel, Noah, and the Tower of Babel are many names you won't read elsewhere. "This man was the father of that man, and lived 800-odd years." The life spans seem incredibly long, with Methuselah topping out at 969 years.

But then you notice something. The long life spans all come before the great flood. After Noah parked the ark, very few people lived more than 120 years.

Interestingly enough, the Sumerian King List, an early record from outside the Bible, mentions various rulers who reigned for thousands of years. The first, A-lulim, was king for 28,800 years. But then it reports, "the Flood . . . swept over the earth," and after that the reigns became dramatically shorter.

ISHMAEL: FATHER OF THE ARABS

ARABS ARE considered children of Abraham, too. They generally trace their ancestry back to Ishmael, Abraham's son by his wife's Egyptian slave, Hagar. Abraham sent the mother and son away from his household at Sarah's request (Genesis 16). Shortly after, God promised Hagar that Ishmael's descendents would make a great nation (Genesis 21:13).

The Quran states that, long before the Temple in Jerusalem, "Abraham and Ismail [Ishmael] built the Kaba [the house of God in Mecca] as the house of God."

MOSES' NAME

*Y*OU MAY KNOW the story of how Moses' mother placed him in a basket and sent it floating down the Nile. Was it her intention all along that the Pharaoh's daughter, bathing nearby, would find Moses and raise him as her own (with the help of his real mother as nursemaid)? We don't know.

In any case, Pharaoh's daughter named the boy Moses, which leads to some interesting wordplay. His Egyptian name was probably Mose or Ramose (*mose* is part of other Egyptian names). But in Hebrew it was Mosheh, which is similar to the word *mashah* ("to draw out"). In fact, in Exodus 2:10, his adoptive mother explains that she drew him out of the water.

Later history provides another pun on the name. God used Moses to draw his people out of slavery.

MOSES AND KING TUT

*H*AVE YOU SEEN or read about the King Tut exhibit that has recently made its way through museums worldwide? The richly supplied tomb of Egyptian boy-pharaoh Tutankhamen was discovered in 1923, and historians ever since have been reveling in its treasures. There are alabaster vessels, gold-covered objects, and furniture inlaid with gold, ivory, and precious stones. The tomb gives us a sense of what life among royalty in ancient Egypt must have been like.

Moses grew up in the Egyptian royal household within 100 years of King Tut. The spectacular furnishings of Tut's tomb represent things Moses probably saw every day. When the Bible says Moses considered the privilege of suffering for God "to be greater wealth than the treasures of Egypt" (Hebrews 11:26), these types of furnishings are exactly what it's referring to.

What's more, most of the ornamentation in the Israelite tabernacle would have had a similar artistic style, because Egyptian-trained artisans crafted it, and the plague-weary Egyptians gave the Israelites gold and valuables when they left for the Promised Land.

WHO WERE THE NEPHILIM?

THE NEPHILIM were ancient men of great stature and reputation, mentioned only in Genesis 6:4 and Numbers 13:33. Little is known about them except that they were very large (the King James Version translates their name as "giants"). When

Israelite spies scouted out the land of Canaan, they reported seeing the Nephilim. Beside these titans, the spies "seemed like grasshoppers."

Where did they come from? Genesis speaks of them as the offspring of "sons of God" and "daughters of humans," but this raises more questions than it answers. It's theologically doubtful that the Nephilim were semi-divine in nature. Could this passage indicate that angels (or demons) were the fathers of this race? Or does it refer to the line of Seth intermarrying with the line of Cain? There is much we don't know about the period between Adam and Noah that it's extremely difficult to speculate.

THE ANAKIM: MEN OF THE NECK

LEAVING EGYPT was tough enough. Wandering through a desert wilderness was no picnic. But then the Israelites had to fight for their place in the Promised Land. They had to dislodge the current residents of Canaan, including several groups of giants.

The major group they kept coming up against were the Anakim (or Anakites), descended from the legendary Nephilim (Numbers 13:33). The term Anakim means "long-necked men" (or possibly "men of the necklace"). They were fearsome warriors. Before the

Israelites entered the land, Moses gave them a pep talk: "You have heard it said of them, 'Who can stand up to the Anakim?' Know then today that the Lord your God is the one who crosses over before you" (Deuteronomy 9:2–3). And under Joshua's leadership, the Anakim were finally vanquished (Joshua 11:21–22).

Among sources outside the Bible, the Egyptian Execration Texts mention three Anakite names. The Israelite town of Hebron derives its name from a noted Anakite warrior, Arba.

THE REPHAIM: SHADY CHARACTERS

*A*T FIRST they seem like just another opponent for the Israelites to tackle on their way to the Promised Land. The Rephaim lived on the eastern side of the Jordan River, and they were defeated as the Israelites came through.

But the Rephaim were also associated with the giant Anakim (see pages 75–76). And so the term is used for various gigantic warriors (2 Samuel 21:16, 18, 20).

Then it gets really odd. The same term, *rephaim*, is used in many of the Old Testament poetic books for the inhabitants of the shady netherworld beyond the grave (Job 26:5). Usually translated as "the dead" or "the shades," the word is also found often outside the Bible in references to those who are dead.

So, was there something otherworldly about the Rephaim warriors, or is it a coincidence that their name was attached to spirits of the dead?

RAMSES II: MONUMENTAL BUILDER

RAMSES II was one of Egypt's greatest pharaohs, reigning for 67 years in the 13th century B.C. Many scholars believe he was the pharaoh who gave Moses such a hard time regarding the Israelites' exodus from Egypt. Ramses II built many great temples, including the astounding temple complex lodged in the sandstone cliffs at Abu Simbel on the Nile River. In the 1960s, when the Aswan Dam threatened this complex, an international rescue effort cut out the temples and relocated them to higher ground.

SATAN AND LUCIFER

THE BIBLE tells us very little about the origins of Satan. Some Bible scholars piece together various passages into a story of a heavenly rebellion and a banishment, but this is not ex-plicitly recorded.

"How art thou fallen from heaven, O Lucifer, son of the morn-ing!" (Isaiah 14:12 KJV). That sounds plain enough, except the term *lucifer* means "light-bringer" and probably refers to the morning star. Outside of this text, the word has no biblical connection with the devil. Isaiah's poetry goes on, describing a ruler's pride and his fall. "You said in your heart, 'I will ascend to heaven; I will raise my throne above the stars of God . . . I will make myself like the Most High.' But you are brought down to Sheol, to the depths of the Pit" (verses 13–15).

It fits the mental picture we have of Satan's story, especially in addition to Jesus' statement, "I watched Satan fall from heaven like a flash of lightning" (Luke 10:18). But Isaiah was specifically referring to the king of Babylon, who was known for his hubris. Of course, many prophetic passages have multiple meanings, so it's possible that this "Lucifer" could also be the devil, but most of our assumptions about Satan's story owe more to Milton's epic poem *Paradise Lost* than to the Bible.

THE ANGEL GABRIEL

FEW ANGELS are named in Scripture. The most famous is Gabriel, but he makes only four appearances. Twice he appeared to Daniel, and in the New Testament, Gabriel made two birth announcements. He told Zechariah the priest about the upcoming birth of his son, John the Baptist, and he announced to Mary that she would bear the Christ child.

The name *Gabriel* means "God is mighty" or "God's mighty one."

MICHAEL, THE ARCHANGEL

ONE OF THE few named angels in Scripture, Michael is described as "a great prince" (Daniel 12:1) and an "archangel" (Jude 1:9). The Epistle of Jude cites an intertestamental legend about Michael's dispute with Satan over the body of Moses.

Michael was apparently less of a messenger (like Gabriel) and more of a warrior. In Revelation 12:7, we read of Michael and his army of angels fighting the great, evil dragon and its forces.

The name *Michael* means "Who is like God?"

THE PHARISEES

ESUS HAD multiple run-ins with the Pharisees. He didn't shy away from criticizing their pride and hypocrisy. Because of this, we see Pharisees as the bad guys in the Gospels, and the word *pharisaical* has come to mean "hypocritical, sanctimonious."

It's sobering to realize that the original impulse of the Pharisees was noble: to follow and obey God's law in every area of life. They tried to inspire others to do the same. Unfortunately, this led to a dry and arrogant legalism in Jesus' time.

THE FIRST *CHRISTIANS*

T MAKES SENSE: A Christian is a follower of Christ. *Christ* is the Greek form of the Hebrew term *messiah*, so more specifically, a Christian is one who believes Jesus is the promised Messiah of the Hebrew Scriptures. The apostles preached this message.

But it took a while for Jesus' followers to take on the name of "Christians." It wasn't until they established a church outside Jerusalem, in Antioch of Syria, that they became known as Christians (Acts 11:26).